A SELECTION OF NONSENSE VERSE

EDWARD LEAR

WITH ILLUSTRATIONS BY THE AUTHOR

HERITAGE

EGMONT

HERITAGE
EGMONT

This selection first published 2014 by Egmont UK Limited
The Yellow Building, 1 Nicholas Road, London W11 4AN
www.egmont.co.uk

ISBN 978 1 4052 7182 0

1 3 5 7 9 10 8 6 4 2

A CIP catalogue record for this title is available from the British Library

Printed and bound in Singapore

55082/1

MIX
Paper
FSC   FSC® C018306

EGMONT LUCKY COIN

Our story began over a century ago, when seventeen-year-old
Egmont Harald Petersen found a coin in the street.

He was on his way to buy a flyswatter, a small hand-operated
printing machine that he then set up in his tiny apartment.

The coin brought him such good luck that today Egmont has
offices in over 30 countries around the world. And that lucky
coin is still kept at the company's head offices in Denmark.

FOREWORD

Edward Lear was born in 1812, the twentieth of twenty-one children. When Lear was still very young, his father suffered financial problems, and so from the age of five Edward's care was entrusted to his eldest sister, Ann, who was more than twenty years his senior.

Although Lear received very little formal education, Ann encouraged his talent for art, and Lear succeeded in making money as a sketch artist from a very young age. His particular skill was for natural history drawings, and by the time he was nineteen he had published a sequence of his own work. *Illustrations of the Family of the Psittacidae, or Parrots* – a collection of twelve lithographic plates – was well received, and captured the attention of Edward Stanley, heir to the Earl of Derby, who would go on to become Lear's patron. Another admirer was Queen Victoria, to whom Lear would later give drawing lessons.

In 1832 Stanley brought Lear to Knowsley Hall in Lancashire, to draw the animals in his family menagerie. During his stays here, Lear would make up funny poems by the score to entertain the Earl's grandchildren, and these provided the inspiration for Lear's first book of poetry,

A Book of Nonsense, which was published in 1846 under the pseudonym Derry down Derry. It contained the one-verse character profiles that we now know as limericks but which Lear called his 'nonsenses', and it was received so enthusiastically that by 1861 Lear was encouraged to release an expanded edition under his own name. This was followed in 1870 by *Nonsense Songs*, which featured many of the longer poems for which he is now best remembered, most notably the evergreen 'The Owl and the Pussy-cat.' By the time of 1872's *More Nonsense* and 1877's *Laughable Lyrics*, Edward Lear was established (and already much cherished) as the father of the nonsense poem.

The critical success of his poetry was always a source of puzzlement to Lear. His later artistic career met with very mixed success, and yet it was his painting that most consumed his thoughts and efforts. Poetry he saw as easy, and fun. 'Nonsense is the breath of my nostrils,' he once wrote. For Lear, writing nonsense was as natural as breathing. Perhaps, then, it was the casualness with which he approached writing his poems – joyful and angst-free as the process was – that made them so irresistibly recitable and memorable, and ensured their genius.

Lear struggled with illness throughout his life, and much of his later adulthood was spent travelling abroad, partly in order to paint the landscapes that would bring him renown as a watercolourist, but also due to his delicate health. He hid the fact that he was epileptic, and this caused him feelings of pain and isolation from his friends. His poems themselves are far from being completely without melancholy. Sadness and loneliness touch even the brightest and noisiest of his nonsense characters: the Dong weaves his luminous nose as he mourns the loss of his Jumbly girl, and the Lady Jingly Jones never recovers from her rejection of the Yonghy-Bonghy-Bò.

But Lear also loved a happy ending, and to his boldest and bravest characters he gave the reward of lasting companionship and high adventure. Who would deny the Quangle Wangle the happiness of being surrounded by the clamorous friends who make their homes in his hat? Or the Nutcrackers and the Sugar-tongs their high-speed escape from drudgery? Ultimately, Lear's poetry championed life's risk-takers – the romantics, the convention-defiers, the misfits and the high-sea sailors.

Lear's final years were spent in San Remo, Italy, with his beloved cat Foss for company. He died in 1888, and he used his last words to speak warmly about the kindness of his many absent friends. His poetry's bittersweet combination of sonorous nonsense and subtle wisdom has spoken to readers across the generations, and continues to speak to us today.

CONTENTS

LIMERICKS

There was a Old Derry down Derry, Who loved to see little folks merry;
So he made them a book, And with laughter they shook,
At the fun of that Derry down Derry.

There was an Old Person of Anerley,
Whose conduct was strange and unmannerly;
   He rushed down the Strand,
   With a Pig in each hand,
But returned in the evening to Anerley.

There was an Old Man with an Owl,
Who continued to bother and howl;
　　He sat on a rail,
　　And imbibed bitter ale,
Which refreshed that Old Man and his Owl.

There was an Old Man of the East,
Who gave all his children a feast;
   But they all ate so much,
   And their conduct was such,
That it killed that Old Man of the East.

There was an Old Person of Basing,
Whose presence of mind was amazing;
   He purchased a steed,
   Which he rode at full speed,
And escaped from the people of Basing.

There was an Old Person of Ems,
Who casually fell in the Thames;
    And when he was found,
    They said he was drowned,
That unlucky Old Person of Ems.

There was an Old Man at a casement,
Who held up his hands in amazement;
   When they said, 'Sir! you'll fall!'
   He replied, 'Not at all!'
That incipient Old Man at a casement.

There was an Old Man of Calcutta,
Who perpetually ate bread and butter;
　　Till a great bit of muffin,
　　On which he was stuffing,
Choked that horrid Old Man of Calcutta.

There was an Old Person of Tring,

Who embellished his nose with a ring;

   He gazed at the moon,

   Every evening in June,

That ecstatic Old Person of Tring.

There was an Old Man of Coblenz,
The length of whose legs was immense;
    He went with one prance,
    From Turkey to France,
That surprising Old Man of Coblenz.

There was an Old Man of Apulia,
Whose conduct was very peculiar;
    He fed twenty sons,
    Upon nothing but buns,
That whimsical Man of Apulia.

There was a Young Lady of Bute,
Who played on a silver-gilt flute;
   She played several jigs,
   To her uncle's white pigs,
That amusing Young Lady of Bute.

There was an Old Person of Mold,
Who shrank from sensations of cold;
So he purchased some muffs,
Some furs and some fluffs,
And wrapped himself well from the cold.

There was an Old Person of Bangor,
Whose face was distorted with anger;
   He tore off his boots,
   And subsisted on roots,
That borascible Person of Bangor.

There was an Old Man of Corfu,
Who never knew what he should do;
  So he rushed up and down,
  Till the sun made him brown,
That bewildered Old Man of Corfu.

There was an Old Person of Dover,
Who rushed through a field of blue clover;
　　But some very large Bees,
　　Stung his nose and his knees,
So he very soon went back to Dover.

There was an Old Man of Leghorn,
The smallest that ever was born;
But quickly snapt up he,
Was once by a Puppy,
Who devoured that Old Man of Leghorn.

There was a Young Person of Smyrna,
Whose grandmother threatened to burn her;
   But she seized on the Cat,
    And said, 'Granny, burn that!
You incongruous Old Woman of Smyrna!'

There was an Old Man who said, 'Hush!
I perceive a young bird in this bush!'
    When they said, 'Is it small?'
    He replied, 'Not at all!
It is four times as big as the bush!'

There was an Old Man with a flute,
A sarpint ran into his boot;
   But he played day and night,
   Till the sarpint took flight,
And avoided that Man with a flute.

There was an Old Person of Sparta,

Who had twenty-five sons and one daughter;

    He fed them on snails,

    And weighed them in scales,

That wonderful Person of Sparta.

There was an Old Man of Whitehaven,
Who danced a quadrille with a Raven;
   But they said, 'It's absurd,
   To encourage this bird!'
So they smashed that Old Man of Whitehaven.

There was an Old Person of Tartary,
Who divided his jugular artery;
 But he screeched to his wife,
 And she said, 'Oh, my life!
Your death will be felt by all Tartary!'

There was a Young Lady whose eyes,
Were unique as to colour and size;
 When she opened them wide,
 People all turned aside,
And started away in surprise.

There was an Old Man who supposed,
That the street door was partially closed;
 But some very large rats,
 Ate his coats and his hats,
While that futile Old Gentleman dozed.

There was a Young Lady of Dorking,
  Who bought a large bonnet for walking;
    But its colour and size,
    So bedazzled her eyes,
That she very soon went back to Dorking.

There was an Old Man of the Nile,
Who sharpened his nails with a file;
    Till he cut off his thumbs,
    And said calmly, 'This comes –
Of sharpening one's nails with a file!'

There was an Old Person of Philae,
Whose conduct was scroobious and wily;
 He rushed up a Palm,
 When the weather was calm,
And observed all the ruins of Philae.

There was an Old Person of Cheadle,
Who was put in the stocks by the beadle;
For stealing some pigs,
Some coats and some wigs,
That horrible Person of Cheadle.

There was an Old Man with a beard,
Who said, 'It is just as I feared! –
   Two Owls and a Hen,
   Four Larks and a Wren,
Have all built their nests in my beard!'

There was an Old Man of Melrose,
Who walked on the tips of his toes;
   But they said, 'It ain't pleasant,
   To see you at present,
You stupid Old Man of Melrose.'

There was an Old Man of the Hague,
Whose ideas were excessively vague;
　　He built a balloon,
　　To examine the moon,
That deluded Old Man of the Hague.

There was an Old Man in a pew,
Whose waistcoat was spotted with blue;
   But he tore it in pieces,
   To give to his nieces, –
That cheerful Old Man in a pew.

There was an Old Man on whose nose,

Most birds of the air could repose;

But they all flew away,

At the closing of day,

Which relieved that Old Man and his nose.

There was an Old Person of Dutton,
Whose head was as small as a button;
　　So to make it look big,
　　He purchased a wig,
And rapidly rushed about Dutton.

There was an Old Person whose habits,
Induced him to feed upon Rabbits;
   When he'd eaten eighteen,
   He turned perfectly green,
Upon which he relinquished those habits.

There was an Old Man of the North,
Who fell into a basin of broth;
   But a laudable cook,
   Fished him out with a hook,
Which saved that Old Man of the North.

There was a Young Lady of Portugal,
Whose ideas were excessively nautical;
   She climbed up a tree,
   To examine the sea,
But declared she would never leave Portugal.

There was an Old Man of the Cape,
Who possessed a large Barbary Ape;
  Till the Ape one dark night,
  Set the house all alight,
Which burned that Old Man of the Cape.

There was an Old Person of Rhodes,
Who strongly objected to toads;
   He paid several cousins,
   To catch them by dozens,
That futile Old Person of Rhodes.

There was an Old Man of the South,
Who had an immoderate mouth;
   But in swallowing a dish,
   That was quite full of fish,
He was choked, that Old Man of the South.

Nonsense Songs

THE OWL AND THE PUSSY-CAT

The Owl and the Pussy-cat went to sea
   In a beautiful pea-green boat,
They took some honey, and plenty of money,
   Wrapped up in a five-pound note.
The Owl looked up to the stars above,
   And sang to a small guitar,
O lovely Pussy! O Pussy, my love,
  What a beautiful Pussy you are,
     You are,
     You are!
What a beautiful Pussy you are!'

Pussy said to the Owl, 'You elegant fowl!
　　How charmingly sweet you sing!
O let us be married! Too long we have tarried:
　　But what shall we do for a ring?'
They sailed away, for a year and a day,
　　To the land where the Bong-tree grows,
And there in a wood a Piggy-wig stood,
　　With a ring at the end of his nose,
　　　His nose,
　　　His nose,
With a ring at the end of his nose.

'Dear Pig, are you willing to sell for one shilling
　　Your ring?' Said the Piggy, 'I will.'
So they took it away, and were married next day
　　By the Turkey who lives on the hill.

They dined on mince, and slices of quince,
  Which they ate with a runcible spoon;
And hand in hand, on the edge of the sand,
  They danced by the light of the moon,
    The moon,
    The moon,
They danced by the light of the moon.

THE JUMBLIES

They went to sea in a Sieve, they did,
   In a Sieve they went to sea:
In spite of all their friends could say,
On a winter's morn, on a stormy day,
   In a Sieve they went to sea!
And when the Sieve turned round and round,
And every one cried, 'You'll all be drowned!'
They called aloud, 'Our Sieve ain't big,
But we don't care a button! we don't care a fig!
   In a Sieve we'll go to sea!'
    Far and few, far and few,
     Are the lands where the Jumblies live;
     Their heads are green, and their hands are blue,
     And they went to sea in a Sieve.

They sailed away in a Sieve, they did,
   In a Sieve they sailed so fast,
With only a beautiful pea-green veil
Tied with a riband by way of a sail,
   To a small tobacco-pipe mast;
And every one said, who saw them go,
'O won't they be soon upset, you know!
For the sky is dark, and the voyage is long,
And happen what may, it's extremely wrong
   In a Sieve to sail so fast!'
     Far and few, far and few,
       Are the lands where the Jumblies live;
       Their heads are green, and their hands are blue,
       And they went to sea in a Sieve.

The water it soon came in, it did,
   The water it soon came in;
So to keep them dry, they wrapped their feet
In a pinky paper all folded neat,
   And they fastened it down with a pin.
And they passed the night in a crockery-jar,
And each of them said, 'How wise we are!
Though the sky be dark, and the voyage be long,
Yet we never can think we were rash or wrong,

While round in our Sieve we spin!'
   Far and few, far and few,
      Are the lands where the Jumblies live;
     Their heads are green, and their hands are blue,
      And they went to sea in a Sieve.

And all night long they sailed away;
   And when the sun went down,
They whistled and warbled a moony song
To the echoing sound of a coppery gong,
   In the shade of the mountains brown.
'O Timballo! How happy we are,
When we live in a sieve and a crockery-jar,
And all night long in the moonlight pale,
We sail away with a pea-green sail,
   In the shade of the mountains brown!'
   Far and few, far and few,
      Are the lands where the Jumblies live;
     Their heads are green, and their hands are blue,
      And they went to sea in a Sieve.

They sailed to the Western Sea, they did,
    To a land all covered with trees,
And they bought an Owl, and a useful Cart,
And a pound of Rice, and a Cranberry Tart,
    And a hive of silvery Bees.
And they bought a Pig, and some green Jack-daws,
And a lovely Monkey with lollipop paws,
And forty bottles of Ring-Bo-Ree,
    And no end of Stilton Cheese.
        Far and few, far and few,
            Are the lands where the Jumblies live;
            Their heads are green, and their hands are blue,
            And they went to sea in a Sieve.

And in twenty years they all came back,
    In twenty years or more,
And every one said, 'How tall they've grown!
For they've been to the Lakes, and the Torrible Zone,
    And the hills of the Chankly Bore!'
And they drank their health, and gave them a feast
Of dumplings made of beautiful yeast;

And every one said, 'If we only live,
We too will go to sea in a Sieve, –
  To the hills of the Chankly Bore!'
    Far and few, far and few,
      Are the lands where the Jumblies live;
      Their heads are green, and their hands are blue,
      And they went to sea in a Sieve.

THE QUANGLE WANGLE'S HAT

On the top of the Crumpetty Tree
   The Quangle Wangle sat,
But his face you could not see,
   On account of his Beaver Hat.
For his Hat was a hundred and two feet wide,
With ribbons and bibbons on every side,
And bells, and buttons, and loops, and lace,
So that nobody ever could see the face
      Of the Quangle Wangle Quee.

The Quangle Wangle said
   To himself on the Crumpetty Tree, –
'Jam; and jelly; and bread;
   Are the best of food for me!
But the longer I live on this Crumpetty Tree,
The plainer than ever it seems to me
That very few people come this way
And that life on the whole is far from gay!'
      Said the Quangle Wangle Quee.

But there came to the Crumpetty Tree,
   Mr and Mrs Canary;
And they said,–'Did ever you see
   Any spot so charmingly airy?
May we build a nest on your lovely Hat?
Mr Quangle Wangle, grant us that!
O please let us come and build a nest
Of whatever material suits you best,
     Mr Quangle Wangle Quee!'

And besides, to the Crumpetty Tree
   Came the Stork, the Duck, and the Owl;
The Snail, and the Bumble-Bee,
   The Frog, and the Fimble Fowl;
(The Fimble Fowl, with a Corkscrew leg;)
And all of them said,–'We humbly beg,
We may build our homes on your lovely Hat, –
Mr Quangle Wangle, grant us that!
     Mr Quangle Wangle Quee!'

And the Golden Grouse came there,
   And the Pobble who has no toes, –
And the small Olympian Bear, –
   And the Dong with a luminous nose.

And the Blue Baboon, who played the flute, –
And the Orient Calf from the Land of Tute, –
And the Attery Squash, and the Bisky Bat, –
All came and built on the lovely Hat
      Of the Quangle Wangle Quee.

And the Quangle Wangle said
   To himself on the Crumpetty Tree, –
'When all these creatures move
   What a wonderful noise there'll be!'
And at night by the light of the Mulberry moon
They danced to the Flute of the Blue Baboon,
On the broad green leaves of the Crumpetty Tree,
And all were as happy as happy could be,
      With the Quangle Wangle Quee.

THE POBBLE WHO HAS NO TOES

The Pobble who has no toes
    Had once as many as we;
When they said, 'Some day you may lose them all;'–
    He replied,–'Fish fiddle de-dee!'
And his Aunt Jobiska made him drink,
Lavender water tinged with pink,
For she said, 'The World in general knows
There's nothing so good for a Pobble's toes!'

The Pobble who has no toes,
    Swam across the Bristol Channel;
But before he set out he wrapped his nose,
    In a piece of scarlet flannel.
For his Aunt Jobiska said, 'No harm
Can come to his toes if his nose is warm;
And it's perfectly known that a Pobble's toes
Are safe, – provided he minds his nose.'

The Pobble swam fast and well,
    And when boats or ships came near him
He tinkledy-binkledy-winkled a bell,
    So that all the world could hear him.
And all the Sailors and Admirals cried,
When they saw him nearing the further side, –
'He has gone to fish for his Aunt Jobiska's
Runcible Cat with crimson whiskers!'

But before he touched the shore,
    The shore of the Bristol Channel,
A sea-green Porpoise carried away
    His wrapper of scarlet flannel.
And when he came to observe his feet,
Formerly garnished with toes so neat,
His face at once became forlorn
On perceiving that all his toes were gone!

And nobody ever knew
 From that dark day to the present,
Whoso had taken the Pobble's toes,
 In a manner so far from pleasant.
Whether the shrimps or crawfish gray,
Or crafty Mermaids stole them away –
Nobody knew; and nobody knows
How the Pobble was robbed of his twice five toes!

The Pobble who has no toes
 Was placed in a friendly Bark,
And they rowed him back, and carried him up,
 To his Aunt Jobiska's Park.
And she made him a feast at his earnest wish
Of eggs and buttercups fried with fish; –
And she said, –'It's a fact the whole world knows,
That Pobbles are happier without their toes.'

THE DONG WITH A LUMINOUS NOSE

When awful darkness and silence reign
  Over the great Gromboolian plain,
    Through the long, long wintry nights; –
When the angry breakers roar
As they beat on the rocky shore; –
    When Storm-clouds brood on the towering heights
Of the Hills of the Chankly Bore: –

Then, through the vast and gloomy dark,
There moves what seems a fiery spark,
    A lonely spark with silvery rays
    Piercing the coal-black night, –
    A Meteor strange and bright: –
Hither and thither the vision strays,
    A single lurid light.

Slowly it wanders, – pauses, – creeps, –
Anon it sparkles, – flashes and leaps;
And ever as onward it gleaming goes
A light on the Bong-tree stems it throws.
And those who watch at that midnight hour
From Hall or Terrace, or lofty Tower,
Cry, as the wild light passes along, –
　　　　'The Dong! – the Dong!
　　　The wandering Dong through the forest goes!
　　　　The Dong! the Dong!
　　　The Dong with a luminous Nose!'

　　　Long years ago
　　The Dong was happy and gay,
Till he fell in love with a Jumbly Girl
　　Who came to those shores one day.
For the Jumblies came in a sieve, they did, –
Landing at eve near the Zemmery Fidd
　　　Where the Oblong Oysters grow,
　　And the rocks are smooth and gray.
And all the woods and the valleys rang
With the Chorus they daily and nightly sang, –

'Far and few, far and few,
 Are the lands where the Jumblies live;
 Their heads are green, and their hands are blue,
 And they went to sea in a sieve.'

Happily, happily passed those days!
       While the cheerful Jumblies staid;
     They danced in circlets all night long,
     To the plaintive pipe of the lively Dong,
       In moonlight, shine, or shade.
For day and night he was always there
By the side of the Jumbly Girl so fair,
With her sky-blue hands, and her sea-green hair.
Till the morning came of that hateful day
When the Jumblies sailed in their sieve away,
And the Dong was left on the cruel shore
Gazing – gazing for evermore, –
Ever keeping his weary eyes on
That pea-green sail on the far horizon, –
Singing the Jumbly Chorus still
As he sat all day on the grassy hill, –

'Far and few, far and few,
Are the lands where the Jumblies live;
Their heads are green, and their hands are blue,
And they went to sea in a sieve.'

But when the sun was low in the West,
    The Dong arose and said; –
    –'What little sense I once possessed
    Has quite gone out of my head!'–
And since that day he wanders still
By lake and forest, marsh and hill,
Singing –'O somewhere, in valley or plain
Might I find my Jumbly Girl again!
For ever I'll seek by lake and shore
Till I find my Jumbly Girl once more!'

Playing a pipe with silvery squeaks,

Since then his Jumbly Girl he seeks,

And because by night he could not see,

He gathered the bark of the Twangum Tree

On the flowery plain that grows.

And he wove him a wondrous Nose, –

A Nose as strange as a Nose could be!

Of vast proportions and painted red,

And tied with cords to the back of his head.

– In a hollow rounded space it ended

With a luminous Lamp within suspended,

All fenced about

With a bandage stout

To prevent the wind from blowing it out; –

And with holes all round to send the light,

In gleaming rays on the dismal night.

And now each night, and all night long,

Over those plains still roams the Dong;

And above the wail of the Chimp and Snipe

You may hear the squeak of his plaintive pipe

While ever he seeks, but seeks in vain

To meet with his Jumbly Girl again;

Lonely and wild – all night he goes, –
The Dong with a luminous Nose!
And all who watch at the midnight hour,
From Hall or Terrace, or lofty Tower,
Cry, as they trace the Meteor bright,
Moving along through the dreary night, –

'This is the hour when forth he goes,
The Dong with a luminous Nose!
Yonder – over the plain he goes;
    He goes!
    He goes;
The Dong with a luminous Nose!'

THE TABLE AND THE CHAIR

Said the Table to the Chair,
'You can hardly be aware,
How I suffer from the heat,
And from chilblains on my feet!
If we took a little walk,
We might have a little talk!
Pray let us take the air!'
Said the Table to the Chair.

Said the Chair unto the Table,
'Now you *know* we are not able!
How foolishly you talk,
When you know we *cannot* walk!'
Said the Table, with a sigh,
'It can do no harm to try,
I've as many legs as you,
Why can't we walk on two?'

So they both went slowly down,
And walked about the town
With a cheerful bumpy sound,
As they toddled round and round.
And everybody cried,
As they hastened to their side,
'See! the Table and the Chair,
Have come out to take the air!'

But in going down an alley,
To a castle in the valley,
They completely lost their way,
And wandered all the day,
Till, to see them safely back,
They paid a Ducky-quack,
And a Beetle, and a Mouse,
Who took them to their house.

Then they whispered to each other,
'O delightful little brother!
What a lovely walk we've taken!
Let us dine on Beans and Bacon!'
So the Ducky, and the leetle
Browny-Mousy and the Beetle
Dined, and danced upon their heads
Till they toddled to their beds.

THE COURTSHIP OF THE YONGHY-BONGHY-BÒ

On the Coast of Coromandel
   Where the early pumpkins blow,
     In the middle of the woods
    Lived the Yonghy-Bonghy-Bò.
Two old chairs, and half a candle, –
One old jug without a handle, –
    These were all his worldly goods,
     In the middle of the woods,
    These were all the worldly goods,
    Of the Yonghy-Bonghy-Bò,
    Of the Yonghy-Bonghy-Bò.

Once, among the Bong-trees walking
  Where the early pumpkins blow,
    To a little heap of stones
  Came the Yonghy-Bonghy-Bò.
There he heard a Lady talking,
To some milk-white Hens of Dorking, –
    ''Tis the Lady Jingly Jones!
    On that little heap of stones
    Sits the Lady Jingly Jones!'
  Said the Yonghy-Bonghy-Bò,
  Said the Yonghy-Bonghy-Bò.

'Lady Jingly! Lady Jingly!
  Sitting where the pumpkins blow,
    Will you come and be my wife?'
  Said the Yonghy-Bonghy-Bò.
'I am tired of living singly, –
On this coast so wild and shingly, –
    I'm a-weary of my life;
    If you'll come and be my wife,
    Quite serene would be my life!' –
  Said the Yonghy-Bonghy-Bò,
  Said the Yonghy-Bonghy-Bò.

'On this Coast of Coromandel,
   Shrimps and watercresses grow,
     Prawns are plentiful and cheap,'
Said the Yonghy-Bonghy-Bò.
'You shall have my chairs and candle,
And my jug without a handle! –
     Gaze upon the rolling deep
     (Fish is plentiful and cheap;)
     As the sea, my love is deep!'
Said the Yonghy-Bonghy-Bò,
Said the Yonghy-Bonghy-Bò.

Lady Jingly answered sadly,
   And her tears began to flow, –
     'Your proposal comes too late,
Mr Yonghy-Bonghy-Bò!
I would be your wife most gladly!'
(Here she twirled her fingers madly,)
     'But in England I've a mate!
     Yes! you've asked me far too late,
     For in England I've a mate,
Mr Yonghy-Bonghy-Bò!
Mr Yonghy-Bonghy-Bò!,

'Mr Jones – (his name is Handel, –
   Handel Jones, Esquire, & Co.)
      Dorking fowls delights to send,
   Mr Yonghy-Bonghy-Bò!
Keep, oh! keep your chairs and candle,
And your jug without a handle, –
      I can merely be your friend!
      – Should my Jones more Dorkings send,
      I will give you three, my friend!
      Mr Yonghy-Bonghy-Bò!
      Mr Yonghy-Bonghy-Bò!

'Though you've such a tiny body,
   And your head so large doth grow, –
      Though your hat may blow away,
   Mr Yonghy-Bonghy-Bò!
Though you're such a Hoddy Doddy –
Yet I wish that I could modi-
      fy the words I needs must say!
      Will you please to go away?
      That is all I have to say –
   Mr Yonghy-Bonghy-Bò!
   Mr Yonghy-Bonghy-Bò!'

Down the slippery slopes of Myrtle,
　Where the early pumpkins blow,
　　To the calm and silent sea
　Fled the Yonghy-Bonghy-Bò.
There, beyond the Bay of Gurtle,
Lay a large and lively Turtle; –
　　'You're the Cove,' he said, 'for me;
　　On your back beyond the sea,
　　Turtle, you shall carry me!'
　Said the Yonghy-Bonghy-Bò,
　Said the Yonghy-Bonghy-Bò.

Through the silent-roaring ocean
　Did the Turtle swiftly go;
　　Holding fast upon his shell
　Rode the Yonghy-Bonghy-Bò.
With a sad primæval motion
Towards the sunset isles of Boshen
　　Still the Turtle bore him well.
　　Holding fast upon his shell,
　　'Lady Jingly Jones, farewell!'
　Sang the Yonghy-Bonghy-Bò,
　Sang the Yonghy-Bonghy-Bò.

From the Coast of Coromandel,
   Did that Lady never go;
      On that heap of stones she mourns
   For the Yonghy-Bonghy-Bò.
On that Coast of Coromandel,
In his jug without a handle,
     Still she weeps, and daily moans;
     On that little heap of stones
     To her Dorking Hens she moans,
   For the Yonghy-Bonghy-Bò,
   For the Yonghy-Bonghy-Bò.

CALICO PIE

Calico Pie,
The little birds fly
Down to the calico tree,
Their wings were blue,
And they sang 'Tilly-loo!'
Till away they flew, –
And they never came back to me!
They never came back!
They never came back!
They never came back to me!

Calico Jam,
  The little Fish swam,
Over the syllabub sea,
  He took off his hat,
  To the Sole and the Sprat,
  And the Willeby-wat, –

But he never came back to me!
  He never came back!
  He never came back!
He never came back to me!

Calico Ban,
  The little Mice ran,
To be ready in time for tea,
  Flippity flup,
  They drank it all up,
  And danced in the cup, –

But they never came back to me!
They never came back!
They never came back!
They never came back to me!

Calico Drum,
The Grasshoppers come,
The Butterfly, Beetle, and Bee,
Over the ground,
Around and round,
With a hop and a bound, –

But they never came back!
They never came back!
They never came back!
They never came back to me!

THE NUTCRACKERS
AND THE SUGAR-TONGS

The Nutcrackers sat by a plate on the table,
    The Sugar-tongs sat by a plate at his side;
And the Nutcrackers said, 'Don't you wish we were able
    Along the blue hills and green meadows to ride?
Must we drag on this stupid existence for ever,
    So idle and weary, so full of remorse, –
While every one else takes his pleasure, and never
    Seems happy unless he is riding a horse?

'Don't you think we could ride without being instructed?
    Without any saddle, or bridle, or spur?
Our legs are so long, and so aptly constructed,
    I'm sure that an accident could not occur.
Let us all of a sudden hop down from the table,
    And hustle downstairs, and each jump on a horse!
Shall we try? Shall we go? Do you think we are able?'
    The Sugar-tongs answered distinctly, 'Of course!'

So down the long staircase they hopped in a minute,
  The Sugar-tongs snapped, and the Crackers said 'crack!'
The stable was open, the horses were in it;
  Each took out a pony, and jumped on his back.
The Cat in a fright scrambled out of the doorway,
  The Mice tumbled out of a bundle of hay,
The brown and white Rats, and the black ones from Norway,
  Screamed out, 'They are taking the horses away!'

The whole of the household was filled with amazement,
  The Cups and the Saucers danced madly about,
The Plates and the Dishes looked out of the casement,
  The Salt-cellar stood on his head with a shout,
The Spoons with a clatter looked out of the lattice,
  The Mustard-pot climbed up the Gooseberry Pies,
The Soup-ladle peeped through a heap of Veal Patties,
  And squeaked with a ladle-like scream of surprise.

The Frying-pan said, 'It's an awful delusion!'
  The Tea-kettle hissed and grew black in the face;
And they all rushed downstairs in the wildest confusion,
  To see the great Nutcracker–Sugar-tong race.

And out of the stable, with screamings and laughter,
    (Their ponies were cream-coloured, speckled with brown,)
The Nutcrackers first, and the Sugar-tongs after,
    Rode all round the yard, and then all round the town.

They rode through the street, and they rode by the station,
    They galloped away to the beautiful shore;
In silence they rode, and 'made no observation,'
    Save this: 'We will never go back any more!'
And still you might hear, till they rode out of hearing,
    The Sugar-tongs snap, and the Crackers say 'crack!'
Till far in the distance their forms disappearing,
    They faded away. – And they never came back!

THE DUCK AND THE KANGAROO

Said the Duck to the Kangaroo,
  'Good gracious! how you hop!
Over the fields and the water too,
  As if you never would stop!
My life is a bore in this nasty pond,
And I long to go out in the world beyond!
  I wish I could hop like you!'
  Said the Duck to the Kangaroo.

'Please give me a ride on your back!'
  Said the Duck to the Kangaroo.
'I would sit quite still, and say nothing but "Quack,"
  The whole of the long day through!

And we'd go to the Dee, and the Jelly Bo Lee,
Over the land, and over the sea; –
   Please take me a ride! O do!'
   Said the Duck to the Kangaroo.

Said the Kangaroo to the Duck,
  'This requires some little reflection;
Perhaps on the whole it might bring me luck,
   And there seems but one objection,
Which is, if you'll let me speak so bold,
Your feet are unpleasantly wet and cold,
   And would probably give me the roo-
   matiz!' said the Kangaroo.

Said the Duck, 'As I sat on the rocks,
   I have thought over that completely,
And I bought four pairs of worsted socks
   Which fit my web-feet neatly.

And to keep out the cold I've bought a cloak,
And every day a cigar I'll smoke,
  All to follow my own dear true
  Love of a Kangaroo!'

Said the Kangaroo, 'I'm ready!
  All in the moonlight pale;
But to balance me well, dear Duck, sit steady!
  And quite at the end of my tail!'
So away they went with a hop and a bound,
And they hopped the whole world three times round;
  And who so happy, – O who,
  As the Duck and the Kangaroo?

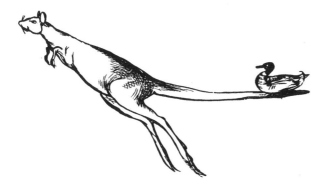

THE SCROOBIOUS PIP

'The Scroobious Pip' remained unfinished at the time of Lear's death in 1888.
It was first published in 1935 and is still less well known than most of
Lear's longer poems. The version reproduced here is as Lear wrote it —
and the incomplete lines are a tempting invitation to readers to try
inventing a few nonsense phrases themselves . . .

The Scroobious Pip went out one day
When the grass was green, and the sky was gray,
Then all the beasts in the world came round
When the Scroobious Pip sat down on the ground.
The Cats and the Dog and the Kangaroo,
The Sheep and the Cow and the Guinea Pig too –
The Wolf he howled, the Horse he neighed,
The little Pig squeaked and the Donkey brayed,
And when the Lion began to roar
There never was heard such a noise before,
And every beast he stood on the tip
Of his toes to look at the Scroobious Pip.

At last they said to the Fox – 'By far
You're the wisest beast – you know you are!
Go close to the Scroobious Pip and say,
"Tell us all about yourself we pray! –
For as yet we can't make out in the least
If you're Fish or Insect, or Bird or Beast." '

The Scroobious Pip looked vaguely round
And sang these words with a rumbling sound –
  'Chippetty Flip – Flippetty Chip –
  My only name is the Scroobious Pip.'

The Scroobious Pip from the top of a tree
Saw the distant Jellybolēē, –
And all the birds in the world came there,
Flying in crowds all through the air.
The Vulture and Eagle – the Cock and the Hen,
The Ostrich, the Turkey, the Snipe and Wren,
The Parrot chattered, the Blackbird sung,
And the Owl looked wise but held his tongue,
And when the Peacock began to scream,
The hullabaloo was quite extreme.
And every bird he fluttered the tip
Of his wing as he stared at the Scroobious Pip.

At last they said to the Owl, – 'By far
You're wisest Bird – you know you are!
Fly close to the Scroobious Pip and say,
"Explain all about yourself we pray! –
For as yet we have neither seen nor heard
If you're Fish or Insect, Beast or Bird!" '

The Scroobious Pip looked gaily round
And sang these words with a chirpy sound –
   'Flippetty chip – Chippetty flip –
   My only name is the Scroobious Pip.'

The Scroobious Pip went into the sea
By the beautiful shore of the Jellybolēē –
All the Fish in the world swam round
With a splashy squashy spluttery sound,
The Sprat, the Herring, the Turbot too,
The Shark, the Sole, and the Mackerel blue,
The ———— spluttered, the Porpoise puffed
————Flounder ————————
And when the Whale began to spout –

——————————

And every Fish he shook the tip
Of his tail as he gazed on the Scroobious Pip.

At last they said to the Whale – 'By far
You're the biggest Fish – you know you are!
Swim close to the Scroobious Pip and say,
"Tell us all about yourself we pray! –
For to know from yourself is our only wish –
Are you Beast or Insect, Bird or Fish?" '

The Scroobious Pip looked softly round
And sang these words with a liquid sound –
  'Plifatty flip – Pliffity flip –
  My only name is the Scroobious Pip.'

The Scroobious Pip sat under a tree
By the silent shores of the Jellybolēē,
All the Insects in all the world
About the Scroobious Pip fluttered and twirled.
Beetles and ——— with purple eyes
Gnats and buzztilential Flies –
Grasshoppers, Butterflies, Spiders too,
Wasps and Bees and Dragonfly blue,
And when the Gnats began to hum
——— bounced like a dismal drum –
And every insect curled the tip
Of his snout, and looked at the Scroobious Pip.

At last they said the Ant, –'By far
You're the wisest Insect – you know you are!
Creep close to the Scroobious Pip and say,
"Tell us all about yourself we pray! –
For we can't find out, and we can't tell why –
If you're Beast or Fish or a Bird or a Fly. –" '

The Scroobious Pip turned quickly round
And sang these words with a whistly sound –
  'Wizziby wip – wizziby wip –
  My only name is the Scroobious Pip.'

Then all the Beasts that walk on the ground
Danced in a circle round and round,
And all the Birds that fly in the air
Flew round and round in a circle there,
And all the Fish in the Jellybolēē
Swam in a circle about the sea,
And all the Insects that creep or go
Buzzed in a circle to and fro –
And they roared and sang and whistled and cried
Till the noise was heard from side to side –
   'Chippetty Tip! Chippetty Tip!
   Its only name is the Scroobious Pip.'

THE PELICAN CHORUS

King and Queen of the Pelicans we;
No other Birds so grand we see!
None but we have feet like fins!
With lovely leathery throats and chins!
   Ploffskin, Pluffskin, Pelican jee!
   We think no Birds so happy as we!
   Plumpskin, Ploshkin, Pelican jill!
   We think so then, and we thought so still!

We live on the Nile. The Nile we love.
By night we sleep on the cliffs above;
By day we fish, and at eve we stand
On long bare islands of yellow sand.
And when the sun sinks slowly down
And the great rock walls grow dark and brown,

When the purple river rolls fast and dim
And the Ivory Ibis starlike skim,
Wing to wing we dance around, –
Stamping our feet with a flumpy sound, –
Opening our mouths as Pelicans ought,
And this is the song we nightly snort; –
   Ploffskin, Pluffskin, Pelican jee!
   We think no Birds so happy as we!
   Plumpskin, Ploshkin, Pelican jill!
   We think so then, and we thought so still!

Last year came out our Daughter, Dell;
And all the Birds received her well.
To do her honour, a feast we made
For every bird that can swim or wade.
Herons and Gulls, and Cormorants black,
Cranes, and Flamingos with scarlet back,
Plovers and Storks, and Geese in clouds,
Swans and Dilberry Ducks in crowds.
Thousands of Birds in wondrous flight!
They ate and drank and danced all night,
And echoing back from the rocks you heard
Multitude-echoes from Bird and Bird, –

Ploffskin, Pluffskin, Pelican jee!
We think no Birds so happy as we!
Plumpskin, Ploshkin, Pelican jill!
We think so then, and we thought so still!

Yes, they came; and among the rest,
The King of the Cranes all grandly dressed.
Such a lovely tail! Its feathers float
Between the ends of his blue dress-coat;
With pea-green trowsers all so neat,
And a delicate frill to hide his feet, –
(For though no one speaks of it, every one knows,
He has got no webs between his toes!)

As soon as he saw our Daughter Dell,
In violent love that Crane King fell, –
On seeing her waddling form so fair,
With a wreath of shrimps in her short white hair.
And before the end of the next long day,
Our Dell had given her heart away;
For the King of the Cranes had won that heart,
With a Crocodile's egg and a large fish-tart.
She vowed to marry the King of the Cranes,
Leaving the Nile for stranger plains;

And away they flew in a gathering crowd
Of endless birds in a lengthening cloud.
 Ploffskin, Pluffskin, Pelican jee!
 We think no Birds so happy as we!
 Plumpskin, Ploshkin, Pelican jill!
 We think so then, and we thought so still!

And far away in the twilight sky,
We heard them singing a lessening cry, –
Farther and farther till out of sight,
And we stood alone in the silent night!
Often since, in the nights of June,
We sit on the sand and watch the moon; –
She has gone to the great Gromboolian plain,
And we probably never shall meet again!
Oft, in the long still nights of June,
We sit on the rocks and watch the moon; –
– She dwells by the streams of the Chankly Bore,
And we probably never shall see her more.
 Ploffskin, Pluffskin, Pelican jee!
 We think no Birds so happy as we!
 Plumpskin, Ploshkin, Pelican jill!
 We think so then, and we thought so still!

THE AKOND OF SWAT

Who, or why, or which, or *what,*

                  Is the Akond of SWAT?

Is he tall or short, or dark or fair?

Does he sit on a stool or a sofa or chair   or SQUAT,

                  The Akond of Swat?

Is he wise or foolish, young or old?

Does he drink his soup and his coffee cold   or HOT,

                  The Akond of Swat?

Does he sing or whistle, jabber or talk,

And when riding abroad does he gallop or walk   or TROT,

                  The Akond of Swat?

Does he wear a turban, a fez, or a hat?

Does he sleep on a mattress, a bed, or a mat   or a COT,

                  The Akond of Swat?

When he writes a copy in round-hand size,
Does he cross his T's and finish his I's   with a DOT,
                                                   The Akond of Swat?

Can he write a letter concisely clear
Without a speck or a smudge or smear   or BLOT,
                                                   The Akond of Swat?

Do his people like him extremely well?
Or do they, whenever they can, rebel   or PLOT,
                                                   At the Akond of Swat?

If he catches them then, either old or young,
Does he have them chopped in pieces or hung   or SHOT,
                                                   The Akond of Swat?

Do his people prig in the lanes or park?
Or even at times, when days are dark   GAROTTE,
                                                   O the Akond of Swat!

Does he study the wants of his own dominion?
Or doesn't he care for public opinion   a JOT,
                                                   The Akond of Swat?

To amuse his mind do his people show him
Pictures, or anyone's last new poem   or WHAT,
                                                   For the Akond of Swat?

At night if he suddenly screams and wakes,
Do they bring him only a few small cakes   or a LOT,
                                                   For the Akond of Swat?

Does he live on turnips, tea, or tripe?
Does he like his shawl to be marked with a stripe   or a DOT,
                                                       The Akond of Swat?

Does he like to lie on his back in a boat
Like the lady who lived in that isle remote,   SHALOTT,
                                                       The Akond of Swat?

Is he quiet, or always making a fuss?
Is his steward a Swiss or a Swede or a Russ   or a SCOT,
                                                       The Akond of Swat?

Does he like to sit by the calm blue wave?
Or to sleep and snore in a dark green cave   or a GROTT,
                                                       The Akond of Swat?

Does he drink small beer from a silver jug?
Or a bowl? or a glass? or a cup? or a mug?   or a POT,
                                                       The Akond of Swat?

Does he beat his wife with a gold-topped pipe,
When she lets the gooseberries grow too ripe   or ROT,
                                                       The Akond of Swat?

Does he wear a white tie when he dines with friends,
And tie it neat in a bow with ends   or a KNOT,
                                                       The Akond of Swat?

Does he like new cream, and hate mince-pies?
When he looks at the sun does he wink his eyes   or NOT,
                                                       The Akond of Swat?

Does he teach his subjects to roast and bake?
Does he sail about on an inland lake   in a YACHT,
                          The Akond of Swat?

Someone, or nobody, knows I wot
Who or which or why or what   Is the Akond of Swat!

Mr and Mrs Discobbolos

Mr and Mrs Discobbolos
      Climbed to the top of a wall,
   And they sat to watch the sunset sky
   And to hear the Nupiter Piffkin cry
      And the Biscuit Buffalo call.
They took up a roll and some Camomile tea,
And both were as happy as happy could be –
      Till Mrs Discobbolos said –
      'Oh! W! X! Y! Z!
      It has just come into my head –
Suppose we should happen to fall!!!!!
            Darling Mr Discobbolos!'

'Suppose we should fall down flumpetty
      Just like pieces of stone!
   On to the thorns, – or into the moat!
      What would become of your new green coat?
      And might you not break a bone?
It never occurred to me before –
That perhaps we shall never go down any more!'

And Mrs Discobbolos said –
'Oh! W! X! Y! Z!
What put it into your head
To climb up this wall? – my own
　　　Darling Mr Discobbolos?'

Mr Discobbolos answered, –
　　'At first it gave me pain, –
　　And I felt my ears turn perfectly pink
　　When your exclamation made me think
　　We might never get down again!
But now I believe it is wiser far
To remain for ever just where we are.' –
　　And Mr Discobbolos said,
　　'Oh! W! X! Y! Z!
　　It is just come into my head –
We shall never go down again –
　　　Dearest Mrs Discobbolos!'

So Mr and Mrs Discobbolos
    Stood up, and began to sing,
  'Far away from hurry and strife
  Here we will pass the rest of life,
    Ding a dong, ding dong, ding!
We want no knives nor forks nor chairs,
No tables nor carpets nor household cares,
    From worry of life we've fled –
    Oh! W! X! Y! Z!
    There's no more trouble ahead,
Sorrow or any such thing –
    For Mr and Mrs Discobbolos!'

THE DADDY LONG-LEGS AND THE FLY

Once Mr Daddy Long-legs,
  Dressed in brown and gray,
Walked about upon the sands
  Upon a summer's day;
And there among the pebbles,
  When the wind was rather cold,
He met with Mr Floppy Fly,
  All dressed in blue and gold.
And as it was too soon to dine,
They drank some Periwinkle-wine,
And played an hour or two, or more,
At battlecock and shuttledore.

Said Mr Daddy Long-legs
   To Mr Floppy Fly,
  'Why do you never come to court?
    I wish you'd tell me why.
All gold and shine, in dress so fine,
  You'd quite delight the court.
Why do you never go at all?
  I really think you *{{o}}{{u}}{{g}}{{h}}{{t}}*!
And if you went, you'd see such sights!
Such rugs! and jugs! and candle-lights!
And more than all, the King and Queen,
One in red, and one in green!'

'O Mr Daddy Long-legs,'
  Said Mr Floppy Fly,
'It's true I never go to court,
  And I will tell you why.
If I had six long legs like yours,
  At once I'd go to court!
But oh! I can't, because *{{m}}{{y}}* legs
  Are so extremely short.

And I'm afraid the King and Queen
(One in red, and one in green)
Would say aloud, "You are not fit,
You Fly, to come to court to a bit!"'

'O Mr Daddy Long-legs,'
   Said Mr Floppy Fly,
'I wish you'd sing one little song!
   One mumbian melody!
You used to sing so awful well
   In former days gone by,
But now you never sing at all;
   I wish you'd tell me why:
For if you would, the silvery sound
Would please the shrimps and cockles round,
And all the crabs would gladly come
To hear you sing, "Ah, Hum di Hum!" '

Said Mr Daddy Long-legs,
   'I can never sing again!
And if you wish, I'll tell you why,
   Although it gives me pain.

For years I cannot hum a bit,
    Or sing the smallest song;
And this the dreadful reason is,
    My legs are grown too long!
My six long legs, all here and there,
Oppress my bosom with despair;
And if I stand, or lie, or sit,
I cannot sing one single bit!'

So Mr Daddy Long-legs
    And Mr Floppy Fly
Sat down in silence by the sea,
    And gazed upon the sky.
They said, 'This is a dreadful thing!
    The world has all gone wrong,
Since one has legs too short by half,
    The other much too long!
One never more can go to court,
Because his legs have grown too short;
The other cannot sing a song,
Because his legs have grown too long!'

Then Mr Daddy Long-legs
   And Mr Floppy Fly
Rushed downward to the foamy sea
   With one sponge-taneous cry;
And there they found a little boat,
   Whose sails were pink and gray;
And off they sailed among the waves,
   Far, and far away.
They sailed across the silent main,
And reached the great Gromboolian plain;
And there they play for evermore
At battlecock and shuttledore.

THE END